Christian and the Great Journey
Copyright © 2022 by Monica Jobe
Illustrated by Judy Anderson Donnelly

Published by Lucid Books in Houston, TX
www.LucidBooks.com

Author headshot by Lois T. Jones

All rights reserved. No part of this publication may be reproduced, stored in a retrieval system, or transmitted in any form by any means, electronic, mechanical, photocopy, recording, or otherwise without the prior permission of the publisher, except as provided for by USA copyright law.

Scripture quotations are taken from the Holy Bible, New International Version®, NIV®. Copyright © 1973, 1978, 1984, 2011 by Biblica, Inc.™ Used by permission of Zondervan. All rights reserved worldwide. www.zondervan.com The "NIV" and "New International Version" are trademarks registered in the United States Patent and Trademark Office by Biblica, Inc.™

eISBN: 978-1-63296-519-6
ISBN: 978-1-63296-517-2 (paperback)
ISBN: 978-1-63296-518-9 (hardback)

Special Sales: Lucid Books titles are available in special quantity discounts. Custom imprinting or excerpting can also be done to fit special needs. Contact Lucid Books at Info@LucidBooks.com

For Stephanie

Enter through the narrow gate. For wide is the gate and broad is the road that leads to destruction, and many enter through it. But small is the gate and narrow the road that leads to life, and only a few find it.

—Matthew 7:13–14

You will seek me and find me when you seek me with all your heart.

—Jeremiah 29:13

Journeys can be long or short,
dangerous or safe,
topsy-turvy,
bumpy, curvy,
and wind a million ways.
Each one is different, just like you, and special in its way.
Use your gifts and figure out which path to take today.

Christian set out on a journey but was feeling rather lost.

He knew he had to find his friend, no matter what the cost.

Christian started on a narrow path with many curves and bends.

He asked a colorful butterfly where this road would end.

"I'm searching for my friend, you see;
he said to take this path."

"You're right," replied the butterfly.
"Keep going; you're on track."

"I started as a caterpillar crawling very slow.

Then somehow, through a miracle, my wings began to grow.

The process wasn't easy, but it was worth it nonetheless.

These colorful wings will carry me to our friend's home to rest."

Christian followed the butterfly, but she was very fast.

She fluttered off ahead, so he continued on the path.

"I mean no harm," the snake lied. "I couldn't help but hear you're searching for your friend's house. You will not find it here."

"I don't know how you missed it—
that big, wide-open gate.

You must have gone right past it."
Then he slithered on his way.

Christian felt confused and pondered what the snake had said.

It couldn't hurt to check things out and find that gate instead.

He thought with all these people, this must be the right way.

The road was far less bumpy; Christian decided he would stay.

Along the road, he saw a sign and on it read, "Dead End."

"That isn't where I want to be. I want to find my friend!"

Christian had a choice to make and quickly turned around.

"I have wasted so much time. How will I find him now?"

Christian heard a gentle voice from somewhere in the trees.

He saw a narrow path and gate and crawled through on his knees.

Relieved, he saw a great big house
and his friend with outstretched hand.

He helped Christian up, smiled, and said,
"Welcome home, my friend."

Monica Jobe grew up in the hometown of Superman, Metropolis, Illinois, where her love of books began early. She currently resides in Clarksville, Tennessee, with her husband of 7 years, Bill; their 6-year-old son, Seth; 13-year-old chocolate lab, Scout; and 3-year-old solid black cat, Freckles (named by Seth). Monica first received the calling to write children's books during an internship in Garden Valley, Texas, following high school. After graduating from the Institute of Children's Literature, Monica set out on her own journey in life and traveled different paths before she could write about the greatest journey of all. She is a Registered Diagnostic Medical Sonographer. Monica is also a music and nature lover who values her family and faith in Jesus most of all.

CPSIA information can be obtained
at www.ICGtesting.com
Printed in the USA
BVHW020947230622
640494BV00007B/302